THE KINGFISHER

playtime

TREASURY

For Poppy, Daisy and Teddy

KINGFISHER
An imprint of Kingfisher Publications Plc
New Penderel House, 283-288 High Holborn
London WC1V 7HZ

First published in hardback by Kingfisher 1989
First published in paperback by Kingfisher 2000
2 4 6 8 10 9 7 5 3 1
1TR/0600/SC/FR/115GPM

This selection copyright © Pie Corbett 1989
Illustrations copyright © Colin and Moira Maclean 1989

A CIP record for this book
is available from the British Library.

ISBN 0 7534 0475 3

Printed in Hong Kong / China

THE KINGFISHER

playtime

TREASURY

A COLLECTION OF PLAYGROUND
RHYMES, GAMES AND ACTION SONGS

SELECTED BY PIE CORBETT

ILLUSTRATED BY MOIRA & COLIN MACLEAN

KING*f*ISHER

ACKNOWLEDGEMENTS

I would like to thank all those who have contributed to this collection: The 92 Primary and Special Schools in East Kent which I visited whilst compiling this anthology and where I often had the privilege to watch children at play and to gather local rules and rhymes; especially the children, staff and community of Lynsted and Norton CPS; Veronica Smith and her class at Briary CPS; the children of Cartwright and Kelsey CEP, Kingsmead CPS, St Stephen's CIS and The Orchard School whose games I collected without them knowing; Eileen Furnell and her class at Blean CPS; Jane Nelson and her class who made me a tape of rhymes from St Peters Methodist PS; Ann Whitley from the Missouri School in the Himalayas; Anne Broomfield from the Pomerang School in Connecticut; Evelyn Bradley from Canada; Anna Budd and her family for Swedish games and rhymes; Gill Batt from the Kent Library Service and Ulla Budd from Faversham Library for their assistance in gathering rhymes from schools and finding me contacts; the Multicultural Centre at Gravesend for advice; Isobelle Duncalfe from Great Chart PS; Bob Fountain and the children of Marslands CPS; Jenny Carter's class for collecting me rhymes and games from Romney Marsh; Ros Norman and her class from Highfield Junior School in Bromley; Robert Hackford for games and songs he collected at Davington CPS, Graveney CPS and from the travelling families of Graveney Marshes; David Townsend for his interest and support; and the children of Colville School, West London. I would like to thank too the many children who demonstrated games, especially Cecilia, Alexis, Claire, Christopher, Marianka, Naima, Madiha, Felix and Saskia. Also the teachers, parents and friends who allowed me to jot down their memories of rhymes and fragments of childhood past. Finally, anyone interested in children's culture owes a debt to the work of Iona Opie and her late husband, Peter, who between them have carried out the most important and exciting work in preserving and giving status to the singing games and lore and language of childhood.

PREFACE

This anthology steals onto children's own territory for these are the rhymes and games of the street, the backyard, the playground and the village. The poetry of playtime links us with our past and reaches out across all nations. You may know these games by different names or with different rules. The game called *Chase*, for example, has over thirty different names in Britain alone and is known as *The Lion* in China and *Touch Tag* in New York. Up to the last moment our youngest advisers were telling us, "Oh no, we don't play it like that any more."

I have tried to present and preserve part of children's culture. Too many children no longer have the opportunity to play together. They live in places where there are no suitable play areas or go to schools that do not allow skipping ropes in the playground. I hope that this book gets tattered and torn in the discovery of playtime. Through their games children begin to learn how to lose, how to play fair, how to co-operate, how to win with grace and how to enjoy the thrill of the game itself. They learn the importance of playing within established rules. In many ways they are finding out how to relate to each other – possibly the most important skill we ever need to learn.

I have had a lot of fun collecting these rhymes and games. I saw intricate dances and heard repetitive songs which reminded me that where the traditions of play and poetry are woven into one they bind us together as a world tribe. The echo of distant voices stirred memories of my own childhood – I hope that you too can rediscover with your children something of that time. For the mystery of poetry and the significance of the game are sheer magic. Any child knows that.

CONTENTS

ACTION RHYMES AND SINGING GAMES 9

A selection of fingerplays, follow my leader games, scary rhymes, counting songs and story rhymes to sing and mime.

DANCING RINGS AND GAMES 23

Traditional and modern singing games danced in a circle.

HAND-CLAPPING RHYMES 37

Familiar songs to clap to, from delightful rhythmic chants to speedy circular hand-clapping games.

DIPPING AND COUNTING-OUT RHYMES 47

Different ways to pick who shall be IT at the start of a game by using the nonsense rhymes and spell-like jingles called dips.

SKIPPING AND BALL-BOUNCING RHYMES 55

Lively songs to skip to individually or in groups as well as ball-bouncing ditties and favourite outdoor ball games.

HIDING, GUESSING, TICKLING AND CHASING 71

Tickling rhymes for younger children, old-fashioned guessing rhymes, intriguing riddles and boisterous hide-and-seek and chasing games of all kinds.

I can do the can-can just like this.
I can do the hoola hoop,
I can do the twist,
Queens go curtsey,
Kings go bow,
Boys go "Hi there!"
Girls go "Wow!"

ACTION RHYMES
AND
SINGING GAMES

Follow the Leader

We are off to Timbuctoo
Would you like to go there too?
All the way and back again,
You must follow our leader then,
You must follow our leader,
You must follow our leader,
All the way and back again,
You must follow our leader.

Follow my Bangalory Man;
Follow my Bangalory Man;
I'll do all that I ever can
To follow my Bangalory Man.
We'll borrow a horse, and steal a gig,
And round the world we'll do a jig,
And I'll do all that I ever can
To follow my Bangalory Man.

Polly Perkin, hold on to my jerkin
   Hold on to my gown,
That's the way we march to town.

☆ *One person is chosen to be the leader and
everyone follows copying his or her actions.*

10

Did you ever see a lassie,
A lassie, a lassie,
Did you ever see a lassie
Who acted like this?
This way and that way,
This way and that way,
Did you ever see a lassie
Who acted like this?

☆ *Mime the actions of the leader.*
Change to LADDIE *if a boy is the leader.*

When I was a baby,
A baby, a baby,
When I was a baby
How happy I was.

Chorus
I was this way, and that way,
That way, and this way,
When I was a baby
Then this way went I.

Verses
When I was a lady,
A lady, a lady,
When I was a lady,
How happy I was.

When I was a sailor,
A sailor, a sailor,
When I was a sailor,
How happy I was.

☆ *Walk or skip while singing the first verse; stop for the*
chorus and mime the verse. Repeat for each verse.

Simple Simon met a pieman,
Going to the fair;
Says Simple Simon to the pieman,
Let me taste your ware.

Says the pieman to Simple Simon,
Show me first your penny;
Says Simple Simon to the pieman,
Indeed I have not any.

SIMON SAYS

Pick one player to be SIMON. Simon then gives orders to the other players such as, "Simon says put your hands in the air." The other players must obey immediately but only if they hear the words "Simon says".

If Simon gives an order without saying, "Simon says" (for example, "Arms out"), any player who obeys the order is out.

If Simon gives an order but does something different (for example, if she says, "Simon says put your hands on your hips" but puts her hands over her eyes), the players who follow the instruction and not Simon are out.

The winner is the one who stays longest in the game. He or she becomes the next Simon.

This old man, he played one,
He played nick-nack on my drum.
Chorus
Nick-nack, paddy-whack,
Give a dog a bone
This old man came rolling home.

☆ *Mime an appropriate action for each
verse. Repeat chorus after each verse.*

Verses

This old man, he played two,
He played nick-nack on my shoe.

This old man, he played three,
He played nick-nack on my knee.

This old man, he played four,
He played nick-nack on my door.

This old man, he played five,
He played nick-nack on my hide.

This old man, he played six,
He played nick-nack on some sticks.

This old man, he played seven,
He played nick-nack up to Heaven.

This old man, he played eight,
He played nick-nack at my gate.

This old man, he played nine,
He played nick-nack on my spine.

This old man, he played ten,
He played nick-nack once again.

Fingerplays

Here is the church,
And here is the steeple,
Open the doors,
And here are the people.

Here is the parson
Going up stairs,
And here is the parson
Saying his prayers.

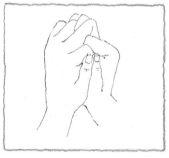

☆ Interlock fingers.

☆ Raise index fingers.

☆ Open thumbs and wriggle fingers.

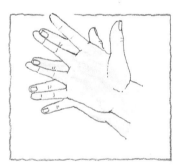

☆ Undo hands. Cross wrists and interlace fingers back to back.

☆ Rotate wrists until palms face each other, fingers curled inside.

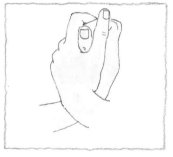

☆ Wriggle thumb.

Snail, snail, put out your horns,
And I'll give you bread and barley corns.

☆ Make a fist, tucking your thumb inside. Lift little finger and index finger to make horns.

Incey wincey spider
Climbing up the spout,
Down came the rain
And washed the spider out.

Out came the sunshine,
Dried up all the rain,
Incey wincey spider
Climbing up again.

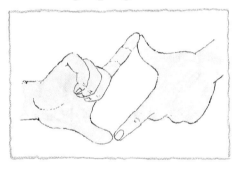

☆ *Climb up by touching opposite thumb and index fingers.*

Peter works with one hammer,
One hammer, one hammer;
Peter works with one hammer,
All day long.

Verses
Peter works with two hammers . . .
Peter works with three hammers . . .
Peter works with four hammers . . .
Peter works with five hammers . . .

☆ *Hammer in time to the verse using one fist, then two, then two fists and one foot, then two fists and both feet. At* FIVE, *fists, feet and head nod to the beat.*

There was a princess long ago,
Long ago, long ago,
There was a princess long ago,
Long, long ago.

☆ *Start by choosing a* PRINCESS, *a* WICKED
FAIRY *and a* PRINCE. *The princess stands
in the centre of a ring. The singing should be
slow until you reach the last verse.*

And she lived in a big high tower,
A big high tower, a big high tower,
And she lived in a big high tower,
Long, long ago.

☆ *The players raise their hands to make a
tower.*

A wicked fairy waved her wand,
Waved her wand, waved her wand,
A wicked fairy waved her wand,
Long, long ago.

☆ *The wicked fairy waves an imaginary wand
over the princess.*

The princess slept for a hundred
    years,
A hundred years, a hundred years,
The princess slept for a hundred
    years,
Long, long ago.

A great big forest grew around,
Grew around, grew around,
A great big forest grew around,
Long, long ago.

☆ *Everyone waves their arms like trees in the wind.*

A gallant prince came riding by,
Riding by, riding by,
A gallant prince came riding by,
Long, long ago.

☆ *The prince rides around the outside of the circle.*

He chopped the trees down one by one,
One by one, one by one,
He chopped the trees down one by one,
Long, long ago.

☆ *He pretends to chop his way through the circle.*

He took the princess by the hand,
By the hand, by the hand,
He took the princess by the hand,
Long, long ago.

☆ *He takes the princess's hand and she wakes up.*

So everybody's happy now,
Happy now, happy now,
So everybody's happy now,
Happy now.

☆ *The circle skips around faster and faster.*

I have a dog and his name is Rags,
He eats so much that his tummy sags,
His ears flip-flop,
And his tail wig-wags,
And when he walks he goes zig-zag.

Chorus
He goes flip-flop, wig-wag, zig-zag,
He goes flip-flop, wig-wag, zig-zag,
He goes flip-flop, wig-wag, zig-zag,
I love Rags and he loves me.
I love Rags and he loves me.

My dog Rags he loves to play
He rolls around in the mud all day.
I whistle but he won't obey,
He always runs the other way.

☆ *Follow the actions using hands and fingers to imitate the words. Hands at either side of head drop forwards for* FLIP-FLOP; *hips wiggle for* WIG-WAG; *arms cross for* ZIG-ZAG; *hands rotate for* ROLLS AROUND; *fingers wiggle for* RUNS THE OTHER WAY *and so on.*

Little Rabbit Foo Foo
Hopping through the green grass,
Scooping up the field mice,
Knocking them on the head.

☆ *Everyone sits in a circle and two players
are chosen to be* RABBIT FOO FOO *and the
GOOD FAIRY. Rabbit Foo Foo hops inside the
circle pretending to scoop up mice. Then the
Good Fairy arrives and gives her a number
of chances.*

Down came the Good Fairy
And she said:
Little Rabbit Foo Foo,
I don't want to see you,
Scooping up the field mice,
Knocking them on the head,
So I'll give you *three* more chances.

☆ *Both verses are repeated with the Good
Fairy appearing each time to count the
number of chances left. When these are used
up the Good Fairy decides what to turn
Rabbit Foo Foo into . . . a monster, a frog . . .?*

Little Rabbit Foo Foo
I really warned you;
Now I'm going to turn you
Into a *red-eyed monster*.

Scary Rhymes

Late on a dark and stormy night,
Three witches stirred with all their might.
Two little ghosts said, "How d'ye do?"
The wizard went tiptoe, tiptoe,
Boooooo!

Poor Willy the Witch
Not too rich,
Had a big itch,
Fell in a ditch,
Poor Willy the Witch.

Hinx, minx, the old witch winks,
The fat begins to fry,
Nobody's home but Jumping Joan,
Father, Mother and I.
Stick, stock, stone dead.
Blind men can't see;
Every knave will have a slave,
You and I must be he.

On a dark, dark night,
In a dark, dark wood,
In a dark, dark house,
In a dark, dark room,
In a dark, dark cupboard,
On a dark, dark shelf,
In a dark, dark box,
There was a GHOST.

Three little ghostesses,
Sitting on postesses,
Eating buttered toastesses,
Greasing their fistesses,
Up to their wristesses.
Oh what beastesses,
To make such feastesses.

I said my pyjamas,
I slipped on my prayers.
I went up my slippers,
I took off my stairs.
I turned off the bed,
I jumped in the light.
The reason for this is
You gave me a fright!

Bat, bat, come under my hat,
    For here's a slice of bacon.
When I bake, I'll give you cake
    If I am not mistaken.

Here we go dancing jingo-ring,
　　Jingo-ring, jingo-ring,
Here we go dancing, jingo-ring,
　　About the merry-ma-tanzie.

Twice about and then we fall,
　　Then we fall, then we fall,
Twice about and then we fall,
　　About the merry-ma-tanzie.

DANCING RINGS AND GAMES

Do you know the Muffin Man,
The Muffin Man, the Muffin Man,
Do you know the Muffin Man
Who lives in Drury Lane?

Yes, I know the Muffin Man,
The Muffin Man, the Muffin Man,
Yes, I know the Muffin Man
Who lives in Drury Lane.

Two of us know the Muffin Man,
The Muffin Man, the Muffin Man,
Two of us know the Muffin Man
Who lives in Drury Lane.

☆ *Choose one player to stand in the middle of a ring. The ring dances around to the first verse, then the player in the centre picks someone who sings the second verse. These two join hands and dance in the middle singing the third verse.*

Repeat the verses changing the number of players until everyone is dancing around singing, "We all know the Muffin Man." The game is for six or more players.

Wallflowers, wallflowers, growing up so high.
We're pretty mermaids and we shall not die.
Except for *Sunita*, she's the only one.
Turn her round, turn her round,
So she cannot face the sun.

☆ *Choose one person to be the caller. Everyone joins hands in a ring and dances around singing. The caller names someone at* EXCEPT FOR *and he or she has to turn around and face outwards. Repeat until everyone has turned around and the whole ring is facing outwards. This ring game is for five or more players.*

Let's go to Kentucky
Let's go to the fair,
To see a señorita,
With flowers in her hair.
Shake it, shake it, shake it,
Shake it if you can;
Oh, rumble to the bottom,
Rumble to the top,
Round and round,
Round and round,
Until you cannot stop.

☆ *At least five players are needed. Choose one to be the* SEÑORITA. *Everyone else dances round her, stopping on* SHAKE. *The Señorita then has to* SHAKE IT *in the middle; on* RUMBLE, *everyone shakes. At the end the Señorita spins round and round with her eyes closed and one arm pointing. Whoever she is pointing at when she stops is the next Señorita.*

☆ An odd number of players is needed for this game. Choose one player to stand in the ring; the others choose partners. On the first verse the player in the middle picks another and they dance together around the outside of the ring. Then they join the circle.

Lou, lou, skip to my lou,
Lou, lou, skip to my lou,
Lou, lou, skip to my lou,
    Skip to my lou, my darling.

Lost my partner, what shall I do?
Lost my partner, what shall I do?
Lost my partner, what shall I do?
    Skip to my lou, my darling.

☆ Now the player whose partner was stolen skips around the outside of the ring.

I've found another one, just like you,
I've found another one, just like you,
I've found another one, just like you,
    Skip to my lou, my darling.

☆ He or she then chooses someone else's partner to dance around with before standing back in the ring. Then the game and the song start again.

The wind blows low, the wind blows high,
The rain comes scattering down the sky.
She is handsome, she is pretty,
She is the girl of the golden city.
So, *Claire West* will you marry me?

If you love him clap your hands,
If you hate him stamp your feet.
The wind blows low, the wind blows high,
The stars are dropping from the sky,
Claire West thinks she'll die,
For want of the golden city.

Now *Tom Saunders* takes her by the hand,
Now he leads her to the water,
Gives her kisses one-two-three-
Mrs *West's* handsome daughter.

☆ *Stand in a ring and choose one dancer to stand in the middle. Her name goes into the last line of the first verse. Decide who she will marry and whisper it round. At the end of the second verse she can clap her hands or stamp her feet. At the start of the third verse put in the name of the dancer she will marry. They dance around together.*

Oats and beans and barley grow,
    Oats and beans and barley grow,
But not you nor I nor anyone know,
    How oats and beans and barley grow.

First the farmer sows his seed,
    Then he stands and takes his ease,
Stamps his feet and claps his hands
    And turns around to view the land.

A-waiting for a partner,
    A-waiting for a partner,
Now open the ring and let one in,
    So oats and beans and barley grow.

☆ *Choose someone to be the* FARMER *in the middle of the ring. Everyone dances around for the first verse. Then the Farmer pretends to* SOW *the seed;* STANDS *with his hands on his hips;* STAMPS *his feet,* CLAPS *and* TURNS *around to look at his land. During the last verse he picks a partner who becomes the next farmer.*

The farmer's in his den,
The farmer's in his den,
E . . . I . . . E . . . I . . .
The farmer's in his den.

Verses

The farmer wants a wife . . .

The wife wants a child . . .

The child wants a nurse . . .

The nurse wants a dog . . .

The dog wants a bone . . .

We all pat the bone . . .

☆ *Choose someone to be the* FARMER *who stands in the middle of a circle. The circle holds hands and moves around clockwise while they sing. The Farmer chooses a* WIFE *and she joins him in the middle. She then chooses a* CHILD *and so on until the* DOG *picks someone to be the* BONE. *If you have lots of players – at least fourteen – the ones in the middle form a new circle that moves around in the opposite direction to the outside circle. On the last verse everyone comes into the middle to pat the poor Bone. The only good thing about being the Bone is that you can be the next Farmer.*

Rosy apple, mellow pear,
    Bunch of roses she shall wear;
Sword and pistol by her side;
    I know who shall be my bride.

Take her by the lily-white hand,
    Lead her across the water,
Blow her a kiss and say goodbye,
    For she's the Captain's daughter.

☆ *Stand in a circle holding hands and choose one dancer to stand in the middle. Everyone dances around singing the first verse. Then the dancer in the middle picks the* BRIDE. *These two then form an arch by holding both hands up high. The circle dancers skip under the arch for the second verse. On the last line the arch comes down capturing someone – he or she has to stand in the middle for the next game. At least five players are needed – the more, the better.*

In and out the windows,
In and out the windows,
In and out the windows,
As we have done before.

Stand and face your partner,
Stand and face your partner,
Stand and face your partner,
As we have done before.

Now follow her to London,
Now follow her to London,
Now follow her to London,
As we have done before.

Bow before you leave her,
Bow before you leave her,
Bow before you leave her,
As we have done before.

☆ *This dance requires at least six dancers who all stand in a circle holding their hands up high to form arches between each other. Choose one dancer to skip in and out of the arches during the first verse. On* STAND AND FACE *he stops by one of the other dancers and waits. During the third verse he follows her in and out of the arches. For the last verse they move to the middle of the ring and bow or curtsey to each other. The partner becomes the next one in the middle and the game is repeated until everyone has had a turn.*

THE HOKEY COKEY

You put your right arm in,
Your right arm out,
Your right arm in,
And you shake it all about.
You do the Hokey Cokey,
And you turn around,
That's what it's all about.

Chorus
Oh, the Hokey, Cokey, Cokey!
Oh, the Hokey, Cokey, Cokey!
Oh, the Hokey, Cokey, Cokey!
Knees bend,
Arms stretch,
Ra! Ra! Ra!

☆ *Any number can play but the song is more fun the more dancers there are. Everyone stands in a circle and follows the actions as they sing the verses. For the chorus everyone joins hands and dances into the middle and out three times; bends knees, stretches out arms and shouts* RA RA RA!

Other verses
You put your left arm in . . .
You put your right leg in . . .
You put your left leg in . . .
You put your whole self in . . .

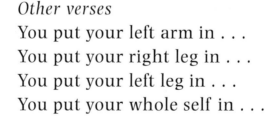

32

PIP, SQUEAK AND WILFRED

At least six players are needed for this rough-and-tumble game. Choose one player to be the caller. Everyone else stands in a circle and the caller moves around naming each player as either a PIP, a SQUEAK or a WILFRED. Once everyone knows who they are the caller stands outside the circle and calls out a name. If she says "Squeak" then all the Squeaks must leave their places and run around the outside of the circle.

The caller can then give two different commands, "Change directions" which means start running in the opposite direction, and "Back home" which means everyone has to race around the circle back to their original places. The last one back is out and sits down.

The caller can shout out "Pip" and "Squeak" at the same time. If she calls out all three then the game can become quite a muddle!

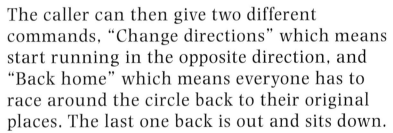

(1)

The big ship sails on the alley, alley O.
The alley, alley O, the alley, alley O.
The big ship sails on the alley, alley O,
On the last day of September.

☆ *At least five dancers are needed but the more the better. Start in a line, holding hands with one dancer standing by a wall with their hand high against the wall to make an arch (1).*

(2)

The Captain said, "This will never, never do,
Never never do, never never do."
The Captain said, "This will never, never do,"
On the last day of September.

☆ *Sing as the dancer at the end of the line leads everyone through the arch (2).*

The big ship sank to the bottom of the sea.
The bottom of the sea, the bottom of the sea.
The big ship sank to the bottom of the sea.
On the last day of September.

(3)

☆ *When the last player passes through the arch the player making the arch will find her arm tugged under her so that she has to twist around and face the other way with her arms crossed and held up (3).*

(4)

☆ *The line now comes back round and through the arch made between the player nearest to the wall and her neighbour (4).*

(5)

We all dip our heads in the deep blue sea.
The deep blue sea, the deep blue sea.
We all dip our heads in the deep blue sea.
On the last day of September.

☆ *When the dancers have been through all the arches and all have crossed arms, they form a ring and sing the last verse – sadly (5).*

See, see, my bonny
I cannot play with you.
My sister's got the mumps,
My brother's got the flu.

Slide down the rainbow,
I'll slam the door.
See you round the back
At half past four.

HAND-CLAPPING RHYMES

Warm-ups

THE ECHO GAME

This is a good way to learn clapping rhythm.
Sit in a circle with one player in the middle.
This player claps out a rhythm on his shoulder,
knee or arm and everyone else must copy.
Any number can play.

THE NAME GAME

Everyone sits in a circle with one player in the
middle. This player claps out the rhythm for a
name and if it is your rhythm you clap it back.
For example:

An – war   Jes – si – ca
Clap clap   clap clap clap

Pat-a-cake, pat-a-cake, baker's man,
Bake me a cake as fast as you can;
Pat it and prick it and mark it with B,
Put it in the oven for baby and me.

☆ *A rhyme to warm up with. Clap your hands together, then your partner's hands.*

Pease porridge hot,
Pease porridge cold,
Pease porridge in the pot,
Nine days old.

Some like it hot,
Some like it cold,
Some like it in the pot,
Nine days old.

 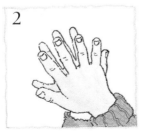  

☆ *This is a basic clapping pattern. Clap your hands together (1); your right hand with your partner's right hand (2); your hands together (1); your left and your partner's left (3); your* hands together (1); finally both your hands and your partner's hands clap together (4). Keep the sequence going smoothly. See also vertical clapping – page 40.

Under the bram bush,
Under the sea, boom boom boom
True love for ever,
True love for me.
When we get married,
We'll have a family,
A boy for you, a girl for me,
Um tiddley um dum, cha-cha!

☆ *Try clapping vertically, right palm upwards*
and left palm downwards for the first beat.

My mammy told me
If I was goody
That she would buy me
A rubber dolly.
My aunty told her
I kissed a soldier
Now she won't buy me
A rubber dolly.

I'm a pretty little Dutch girl,
As pretty as can be be be.
And all the boys in the football team
Go crazy over me me me.
My boyfriend's name is Tony,
He comes from macaroni,
He's got 48 toes and a cherry on his nose
And this is how my story goes:
My boyfriend gave me an apple,
My boyfriend gave me a pear.
My boyfriend gave me 25 cents
To kiss him on the stairs stairs stairs.
I gave him back the apple,
I gave him back the pear,
I gave him back the 25 cents
And threw him down the stairs stairs stairs!

☆ *Clap three times on your knees for*
the repeated words. Here are more verses
if you can keep the rhythm going!

One day when I was walking
I heard my boyfriend talking
To the prettiest girl
With a strawberry curl,
And this is what she said:
I L-O-V-E love you,
I K-I double S kiss you.
But she jumped in a lake
And swallowed a snake
And went home
With a belly ache.

Miss Mary Mack,
      Mack,
      Mack,
All dressed in black,
      black,
      black,
With silver buttons,
      buttons,
      buttons,
All down her back,
      back,
      back,
She asked her mother,
      mother,
      mother,
For fifteen cents,
      cents,
      cents,
To see the elephant,
      elephant,
      elephant,
Jump over the fence,
      fence,
      fence.
He jumped so high,
      high,
      high,
He reached the sky,
      sky,
      sky,
And never came back,
      back,
      back,
Till the first of July,
      ly,
      ly.

☆ *For each verse: Touch knees, touch shoulders, clap hands together; then clap your partner's hands three times. Spin around at the end.*

I had a little monkey,
I called him Sonny Jim,
I put him in a bath tub,
To see if he could swim;

He drank all the water,
He ate up all the soap,
He lay down on the bath mat,
Blowing bubbles from his throat.

"Mummy, Mummy, I feel ill,
Call the doctor down the hill."
In came the doctor, in came the nurse,
In came the lady with the alligator purse.

"He's naughty," said the doctor,
"He's wicked," said the nurse,
"Hiccups!" said the lady with the alligator purse.

Out went the doctor, out went the nurse,
Out went the lady with the alligator purse.

Dom dom malayas,
Sweet sweet malayas,
Sweet sweet lady,
Gimme, gimme chocomilk,
Chocomilk is out.
One, two, three.

☆ *This is a very fast clapping game. Stand in a circle and choose someone to begin. He swings his right hand to clap the left hand of the player standing on his left. That player swings her right hand to the left and so on around the circle. The player whose hand is clapped on* THREE *is out of the game and the rhyme is repeated until only two players are left. These two players hold hands and rotate their wrists until* OUT. *Now the player whose hand is uppermost strokes the other's hand for* ONE *and* TWO *and tries to slap it on* THREE. *The player whose hand is being stroked can snatch his or her hand away to avoid the slap!*

WHO STOLE THE COOKIES?

All players:	Who stole the cookie from the cookie jar?
	Number One stole the cookie from the cookie jar.
Number One:	Who, me?
All players:	Yes, you.
Number One:	Not I.
All players:	Then who?
	Who stole the cookie from the cookie jar?
Number One:	Number Eight stole the cookie from the cookie jar.
Number Eight:	Who, me?
All players:	Yes, you.
Number Eight:	Not I.
All players:	Then who?
	Who stole the cookie from the cookie jar?
Number Eight:	Number Five stole the cookie from the cookie jar.

☆ *Up to ten players can join in this game. They sit in a circle and everyone picks a number for themselves – a different number from one to ten. Everyone claps their own hands and their neighbour's hands alternately, and chants the words. The player who is number One picks the number of another player. This player has to quickly continue by choosing another number. He or she can say any number so long as it hasn't already been picked. If it has, the player calling the number is out.*

Each peach pear plum
I spy Tom Thumb.

Tom Thumb fast asleep
I spy Bo-Peep.

Bo-Beep round the corner
I spy Jack Horner.

Jack Horner up a pole
I spy King Cole.

King Cole drinking juice
I spy Mother Goose.

Mother Goose gave a shout
That means you are OUT.

DIPPING AND COUNTING-OUT RHYMES

For many games you need to choose one player
to be IT. There are lots of ways to do this.

You can call out, "Last
off the ground is it." . . .

. . . or, "Last to the
lampost is it."

You can make a circle with your
arms and call, "Last in the bucket
is it." The last player to put
his hands into the circle is IT.

Or you can dip – use a rhyme to count people out.
All the players stand in a circle or line and one
player points to the others in turn saying the words.
The dip can pick IT straightaway:

The one who gets to number two
Surely must be it – one, TWO!

Or the rhyme can count players out and
the last one left is chosen:

Red, white and blue,
The cat's got flu,
The dog's got chicken pox,
And out goes YOU!

☆ *Three ways to count out with a rhyme.*

Eeny meeny miny mo
Catch a baby by the toe.
If he squeals let him go
Eeny meeny miny mo.

☆ *By pointing at each player.*

One potato
Two potato
Three potato
Four –
Five potato
Six potato
Seven potato
More.

☆ *By counting fists.*

Your shoes are dirty,
Your shoes are clean,
Your shoes are not fit
To be seen by the Queen.

☆ *By counting feet.*

Intery, mintery, cutery, corn,
Apple seed and briar thorn.
Wire, briar, limber lock,
Five geese in a flock.
One flew East and one flew West,
One flew over the cuckoo's nest.
O-U-T spells out.

Inky pinky ponky
Daddy bought a donkey.
The donkey died,
Daddy cried,
Inky pinky ponky.

Ip dip dip,
My blue ship,
Sailing on the water
Like a cup and saucer.
Ip dip dip.

Icker backer,
Soda cracker,
Icker backer boo,
Engine number nine,
Out goes you.

Ipper dipper dation,
My operation.
How many people at the station?

☆ *The last player pointed at gives a number, for example,* FIVE.

The one who comes to number FIVE
Will surely not be IT.
1, 2, 3, 4, 5.

Engine, engine, number nine,
Running up Chicago line.
If the train goes off the track
Do you want your money back?
Yes, no, maybe so.

☆ *The player landed on says* YES *or* NO, *for example,* YES.

Y-E-S spells yes
So out you must go.

Ibble wobble black bobble,
Ibble wobble out,
Turn the dirty dish cloth
Inside out –
First you turn it inside,
Then you turn it out –
Ibble wobble black bobble,
Ibble wobble out.

Eeny meeny macker racker
Rari rie domi nacker
Chicker bocker lolli popper
Om pom push
Alli galli goo
Out goes you.

Eachie, peachie, pear, plum,
When does your birthday come?
One, two, three, you are out.

☆ *The last player pointed at says his or her birthdate – for instance the 3rd of April – and the rhyme continues using the number given.*

I climbed up the apple tree,
All the apples fell on me.
Bake an apple, bake a pie,
Have you ever told a lie?

NO.

Yes you did, you know you did,
You broke your Mother's tea-pot lid.
What colour was it?

☆ *The player pointed at last chooses
a colour, for example, blue, and the rhyme
continues.*

No it wasn't, it was gold,
That's another lie you've told.
Out you go for saying so.

My mother bought a dress –
What colour do you guess?

☆ *The player pointed at suggests a colour,
for example, red, and the rhyme continues:*

R-E-D spells red.
Out you go
For saying so.

Drip drop, drip drop,
    down by the sea.
Up popped a mermaid,
    she said to me:
"Skip in the middle,
    one at each end,
Each is a sister,
    each is a friend."

SKIPPING AND BALL-BOUNCING RHYMES

Warming-up Rhymes

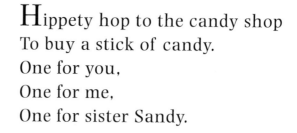

Hippety hop to the candy shop
To buy a stick of candy.
One for you,
One for me,
One for sister Sandy.

☆ *Mark two lines on the ground with skipping ropes. Hop from one to the other. Widen the gap little by little.*

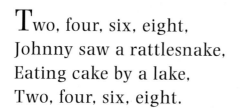

Two, four, six, eight,
Johnny saw a rattlesnake,
Eating cake by a lake,
Two, four, six, eight.

☆ *Lay the skipping rope on the ground like a snake. Try to walk along its back.*

Jack be nimble,
Jack be quick,
Jack jump over
The candlestick.

☆ *Practise jumping over objects.*

Roly poly,
Barley Sugar.

☆ *Without a rope practise skipping from one leg to the other. Sing as you skip.*

Andy Pandy,
Sugary Candy,
French Almond,
Nuts!

☆ *Start skipping slowly and see how quickly you can go.*

Under the stars
Over the moon.

☆ *The rope is held by two players – the enders – who move it up and down chanting the rhyme. On* UNDER *the players run under the rope; on* OVER *they jump over it.*

Early in the morning at half past eight,
I heard the postman knocking at the gate,
Up jumps *Lucy* to open the door
How many letters fell on the floor?
1, 2, 3, 4, 5 . . .

Who from?
A-B-C-D-E . . .

☆ *Two people hold the rope.
After* JUMPS, *they name a friend
who skips until she trips. She
skips until she stumbles on a
number which tells her how
many letters she received.
Skip on to find the initial of the
person who sent the letters.*

I'm a girl guide, dressed in blue,
Here are the actions I must do.
Salute to the captain,
Bow to the Queen,
Turn right round
And count sixteen.
1, 2, 3, 4, 5 . . . 16.

☆ *Two people swing the rope while
the skipper copies the actions of
the rhyme.*

Lemon pie, apple tart.
Tell me the name of your sweetheart.
A-B-C-D-E-F . . .

Felix is your love
White doves above,
Sitting on his knee
Under the apple tree,
Kissing 1, 2, 3, 4 . . .

☆ *Skip this game to find out who you will marry! The skipper skips until she trips. Then her friends choose someone she knows whose name begins with that letter, for example,* F FOR FELIX. *Then she skips again to find out how many kisses she gets!*

Underneath the apple tree
A boy said to me –
Kiss me, cuddle me,
Who should it be?
A-B-C-D . . .
Will you get married?
Yes, No, Yes, No . . .
What will he marry you in?
Silk, satin, cotton, rags . . .
How will you go to your wedding?
Coach, carriage, wheelbarrow, car . . .
How many children?
1, 2, 3, 4, 5 . . .

☆ *Two people hold the rope and everyone takes it in turns to find out their future.*

I went to the animal fair,
The birds and the beasts were there.
By the light of the moon the gay baboon
Was combing his golden hair.
The monkey fell out of his bunk
And slid down the elephant's trunk.
The elephant sneezed
And fell on his knees
And what became of the monkey,
Monkey, monkey,
Monkey, monk!

☆ *Two players swing the rope. Everyone skips in.*
Anyone who makes a mistake is out. Skip on
until only one person is left in.

Not last night
But the night before
Twenty-four robbers
Came knocking at my door.
Went downstairs to let them in
And this is what I saw:

Spanish lady, Spanish lady
Do high kicks.

Spanish lady, Spanish lady,
Take a bow.

Spanish lady, Spanish lady,
That's all for now.

☆ *Two players swing the rope. Everyone takes it in turns to skip in, in pairs, and do the actions.*

Ball-bouncing

Solid rubber balls are best for bouncing games.

Bounce the ball on the ground and pat it down again.

Or bounce the ball against a wall and catch it.

Try putting the ball inside the toe of an old stocking or one half of a pair of tights. Bounce the ball from side to side against a wall.

Chant a rhyme as you bounce or
catch the ball.

Bouncie, bouncie ballie,
My friend Paulie,
I gave her a slap,
She gave me one back,
Bouncie, bouncie ballie.

Mickey Mouse came to my house
I asked him what he'd like –
A sunset smile,
A crocodile,
A ride upon my bike.

One, two, three,
Mother caught a flea,
She salted it and peppered it
And served it up for tea!

Types of Bounces

Here are ten ways to bounce a ball
against a wall.

Overs
Throw the ball overarm
or straight at a wall.

Unders
Throw the ball underarm
or under your leg.

Dropsies
Throw the ball against
a wall and let it bounce
on the ground before
catching it.

Bouncies
Bounce the ball on
the ground once and
catch it as it comes
off the wall.

Backsies
Throw the ball
against a wall from
behind your back,
turn around, catch.

Onesies
Catch the ball with one hand.

Twosies
Catch the ball with two hands.

Turnsies
Throw the ball against a wall, spin right around and catch it.

Clapsies
Throw the ball and clap once before catching it.

Stampsies
Throw the ball and stamp your feet once before catching it.

Big black bug
Sitting on a rug –
I one it,
I two it,
I three it,
I four it,
I five it,
I six it,
I seven it,
You ate it!

☆ *In this game, you have to try seven different*
kinds of bounces – without dropping the ball.

PIGGY-IN-THE-MIDDLE

You need three people but you can play with more. Dip (see page 48) to decide who will be PIGGY and stand in the middle. Piggy then has to try to catch the ball as the others throw it backwards and forwards.

SCORE THROW

Any number can play this ball game. Chalk some shapes on a wall and write a number – the score – inside each one. Give the smaller shapes a higher score. Everyone stands back from the wall behind a line drawn on the ground. No one is allowed over the line. Everyone has three turns to throw the ball against the wall and score as much as they can.

HOOP CATCH

You need four players for this game. Two stand in the middle and hold a hoop between them. The others stand on either side and throw the ball backwards and forwards through the hoop. If someone drops it they have to take a turn holding the hoop.

DEAD DONKEYS

Any number can play. Everyone stands in a circle and throws the ball around. If anyone drops the ball they say the letter D. If the same person misses again they say the letter O. If they miss a third time they say the letter N, then K, E and Y. When they have spelt out D-O-N-K-E-Y they are out. The last one left wins. The others are DEAD DONKEYS.

QUEENIE

This guessing game is for five or more players. Start by dipping (see pages 48–49) to choose who will be QUEENIE. She turns her back on the other players and throws the ball over her shoulder. The player nearest the ball picks it up and hides it behind his back. When Queenie turns around everyone sings:

Queenie, Queenie, who's got the ball?
Is she big or is she small?
Is she fat or is she thin?
Or is she like a rolling pin?

Queenie then runs around the players looking for the ball. But they spin around so she can't see who has it.

Queenie then guesses who has the ball by pointing at someone and they have to show their hands one by one and say, "I've not got it." If she guesses right the first time she carries on as Queenie. If she doesn't then the player with the ball becomes Queenie.

Girls and boys come out to play,
The moon doth shine as bright as day.
Leave your supper and leave your sleep,
Come join your playfellows in the street.
Come with a whoop and come with a call,
Come with a good will or not at all.
Up the ladder and down the wall,
A half-penny loaf will serve us all;
You will find milk, and I'll find flour,
And we'll have a pudding in half an hour.

HIDING, GUESSING, TICKLING AND CHASING

Peek-a-boo, peek-a-boo,
Who's that hiding there?
Peek-a-boo, peek-a-boo,
    Tom's behind the chair.

☆ *Change the name* TOM *to that of the person you are playing with.*

Handy dandy,
Riddledy ro.
Which hand will you have,
High or low?

☆ *Start by hiding a small object in one clenched fist. The other player has to guess which hand it is in. If she guesses correctly, it is her turn to hide the object; otherwise she must guess again.*

Hurly burly trump a tray
    The goat was bought on market day.
Peter Piper hunt a buck.
    How many horns now stand up?

☆ *One player covers his or her eyes while the other holds up a number of fingers and chants the rhyme. The game is to guess the number of fingers held up.*

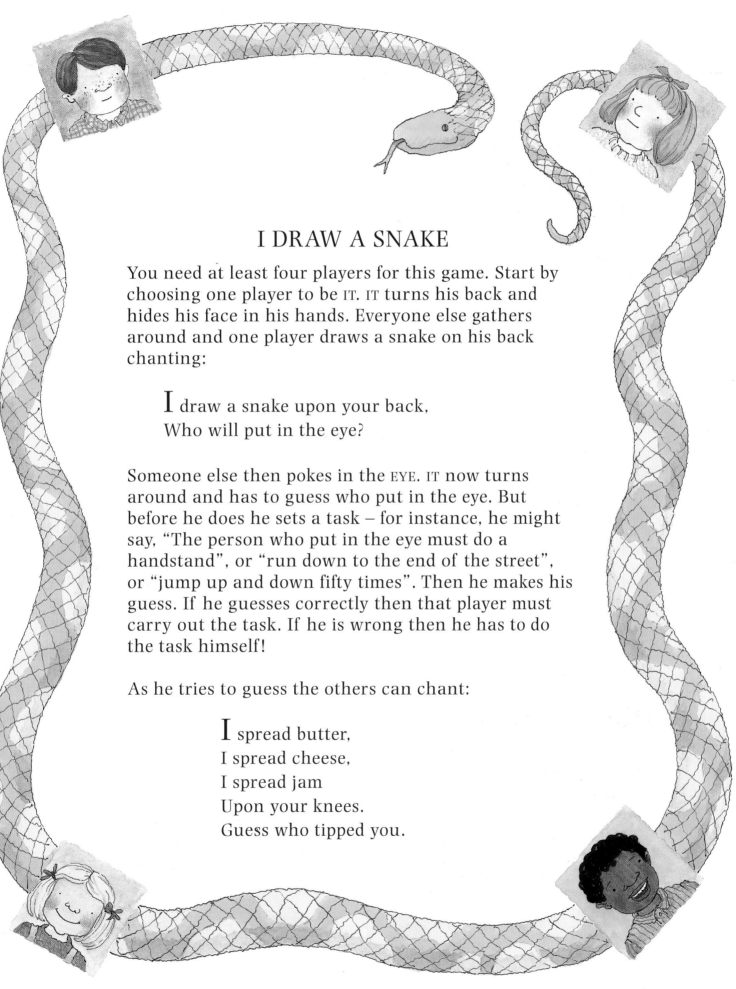

I DRAW A SNAKE

You need at least four players for this game. Start by choosing one player to be IT. IT turns his back and hides his face in his hands. Everyone else gathers around and one player draws a snake on his back chanting:

> I draw a snake upon your back,
> Who will put in the eye?

Someone else then pokes in the EYE. IT now turns around and has to guess who put in the eye. But before he does he sets a task – for instance, he might say, "The person who put in the eye must do a handstand", or "run down to the end of the street", or "jump up and down fifty times". Then he makes his guess. If he guesses correctly then that player must carry out the task. If he is wrong then he has to do the task himself!

As he tries to guess the others can chant:

> I spread butter,
> I spread cheese,
> I spread jam
> Upon your knees.
> Guess who tipped you.

Hide

HIDE-AND-SEEK

Play this game with as many people as possible. The player who is IT closes her eyes and counts up to twenty or more while everyone else scatters and hides. When she reaches twenty, she shouts, "Coming – ready or not." The last player to be found is the winner.

Seek

BUG IN THE RUG

In this game if you are found you can run for "home". If you get there without being touched then you are safe.

CUCKOO

In this game only one player hides and everyone else seeks.

TOAD IN THE HOLE

In this game if you are found then you join in looking for the others.

CRANEY CROW

Chickamy, chickamy, craney crow,
I went to the well to wash my toe.
When I got back, my chickens were gone.
What time is it, Old Witch?
One o'clock, two o'clock, three . . .

☆ *The seeker is the* WITCH *and the others are the* CHICKENS *and they hide while the rhyme is chanted and the hours one to twelve are counted. Then the Witch looks for the Chickens.*

SARDINES

Any number of people can play this game and it is best played indoors where there are lots of good places to hide. One player is chosen to be the SARDINE and he goes off to hide. After a while everyone splits up to look for him. If they find the Sardine then they hide with him. It can become quite a squash!

The last player to find the Sardine is the loser and has to begin the next game. Sometimes *Sardines* is called *Squashed Tomatoes*.

KICK THE CAN

Play this game with as many people as possible. If you don't have a tin-can, a lump of wood or a stone will do. The tin-can is placed on the ground as the home base. Using a dip (see pages 48–49), choose a player to be IT.

IT kicks the can hard and while he is putting it back on the base everyone else scatters and hides.

123 I see Lisa.

IT then searches and if he sees anyone hiding he can capture them by putting his foot on the can and calling their name.

The players who are captured have to stand by the base and can be released only by a free player running up and kicking the can away.

Ticklers

Can you keep a secret?
I don't suppose you can.
You mustn't laugh or smile
While I tickle your hand.

Davy, Davy, Dumpling
Boil him in the pot.
Sugar him and butter him,
Eat him while he's hot.

☆ *Change the name* DAVY *to that of the person you are tickling.*

☆ *An unusual traditional toe counting – and tickling – rhyme.*

This little pig had a rub-a-dub,
This little pig had a scrub-a-scrub.

Criss, cross
Applesauce,
Spiders climbing up your back.
Cool breeze,
Tight squeeze,
And now you've got the shivers.

☆ *Sketch a cross for* CROSS;
tickle back for SPIDERS; *blow*
for the BREEZE; *hug for* SQUEEZE;
and shake gently on SHIVERS.

Bears!

This little pig-a-wig ran upstairs,
This little pig-a-wig called out, "Bears!"

Down came the jar with a loud slim slam!
And this little pig had all the jam.

The simplest way to play touch chase is for the person who is IT to touch another player and then he or she becomes IT. Choose who will be IT by using a dip (see page 48).

Cowboy Joe from Mexico.
Hands up, stick 'em up!
Don't forget to pick 'em up.
O-U-T spells out!

In these games the rules are all different.

1

Tunnel Touch
When you are caught put one arm against something to make a tunnel. If someone else runs under your arm, you are free.

2

Ticky Leapfrog
If you are touched you crouch down. When someone leapfrogs over you, you are free.

3

Off-ground Tiggy
You are safe from being touched by finding a place that is off the ground – but you are not allowed to stay there too long!

4

Colours
Everyone decides on a colour. If you are touching that colour then you are safe.

5

Shadow Tick
This time you catch someone by touching their shadow with your foot. It doesn't count if you touch *them* at all!

6

Three Squat Tag
If you are about to be caught you can bob down and touch the ground. Then you are safe. But you can only do this three times in a game!

7

Stick-in-the-Mud
If you are touched you are frozen to the spot like a statue. When another player touches your hand, you are free.

8

Touch Wood or Iron
If you are touching wood or iron then you are safe.

9

Underground He
If you are caught stand with your legs open wide. If someone crawls under your legs, you are free.

POISON

This game is for three or more players. One player is chosen to be IT and she holds out her hands. Everyone else holds onto a finger. IT says, "I went to the moon and bought some . . ." and she lists foods beginning with the letter p, such as peas or pancakes. But if she says POISON everyone has to run for it. She chases after them and the player who is caught becomes IT. If a player lets go and starts running before IT says POISON then he is out before the game has even started!

SHOPS

At least four people are required for this game. One player is chosen to be MOTHER and she tells her children (everyone else) that she is going to the shops. She gives each of them a job to do while she is away, for example, sweeping, cleaning, tidying, mowing the lawn and digging the garden. Then she pretends to go to the shop and all the children creep up to listen to what she is going to buy. Mother says out loud all the things she is buying. For example, "I'd like to buy a . . . new coffee-pot, a plate, some bananas . . ." She buys a number of different things until suddenly she says, "I'd like to buy a . . . feather to tickle my children with!"

Everyone runs for it! The player who is caught is the next MOTHER.

WHAT'S THE TIME, MR WOLF?

You need at least five people – the more that play the better. One person is chosen to be MR WOLF.

Mr Wolf walks around and everyone else follows – at a safe distance – calling, "What's the time, Mr Wolf?" Mr Wolf replies, "One o'clock" or "Two o'clock" and so on until suddenly he shouts, "Dinner time – and I'm coming to get you!"

And with that he chases after everyone. You can only escape if you make it to your home base. But the player who is caught becomes the next Wolf.

GLUEPOTS

A game for as many people as possible. One player is chosen to be IT and has to chase the others. Before the game starts IT picks a number of special places to put the people she catches. These are her GLUEPOTS and once someone is put there they cannot move. They can be released only if a free player touches their hand – but if the free player makes a mistake and puts a foot into the Gluepot then he or she is stuck there too!

RED LION

You need at least four players. One player is chosen to be IT – the LION. The Lion has a den. Everyone else has a home base as far away as possible from the Lion's den. The players chant:

> Red Lion, Red Lion,
> Come out of your den.
> Whoever you catch
> Can be one of your men.

The Lion chases everyone and they all have to run for their home base to be safe. If the Lion touches anyone three times before they get home then he can take them back to his den. They then become Lions too.

FARMER, FARMER

At least four players are required but the more that play the better. One player is chosen to be the FARMER. Everyone else lines up in front of him or her and calls out: "Farmer, Farmer, may we cross your golden river?" The Farmer replies, picking a colour: "Only if you have *red*."

Anyone wearing this colour can cross safely. The others have to dash across the river. If the Farmer catches them then they are out.

☆ *Some alternative ways to ask to cross the river.*

Old Mother Witch, may we cross your ditch?

Farmer, farmer, may we pass over the hills and over the grass?

Please Mr Crocodile, may we cross the water in a cup and saucer upside-down?

Please Mr Porter, may we cross your golden water to see your fairy daughter drink a cup of water?

FOX IN THE WALL

This game is for six or more players. One player is chosen to be the FARMER, one player is the FOX and all the others are GEESE. The Farmer leaves the Geese and goes far away. The Fox finds a place to hide between the Farmer and the Geese. This is his den.

The Farmer calls: "Geese, geese, come home."

GEESE: "We are frightened."
FARMER: "What of?"

GEESE: "The Fox."
FARMER: "The Fox has gone away
            and won't be back today.
            Geese, geese, come home."

The Geese then run towards the Farmer and the Fox tries to catch one and take it back to his den.

CROWS AND CRANES

This game is for two teams with at least five players on each team. There is also a caller. One player is chosen to be the caller and stands in the middle. Everyone else splits up into the teams called CROWS and CRANES. The Crows stand at one end of the room or garden and the Cranes stand at the opposite end.

When they are ready, the caller shouts, "Start walking!"

Both teams march towards the middle. As they get closer the caller calls out the name of one of the teams – Crows or Cranes. Whichever team is named has to chase the others and try to touch them before they get back to their home base. The players who are caught have to join the other side and the team with the largest number wins. The caller can make things more interesting by keeping each side waiting to know which team will be called, "Crrrrr . . . anes!"

You could also play *Rats and Rabbits*, *Black and Blue*, or *Crusts and Crumbs*.

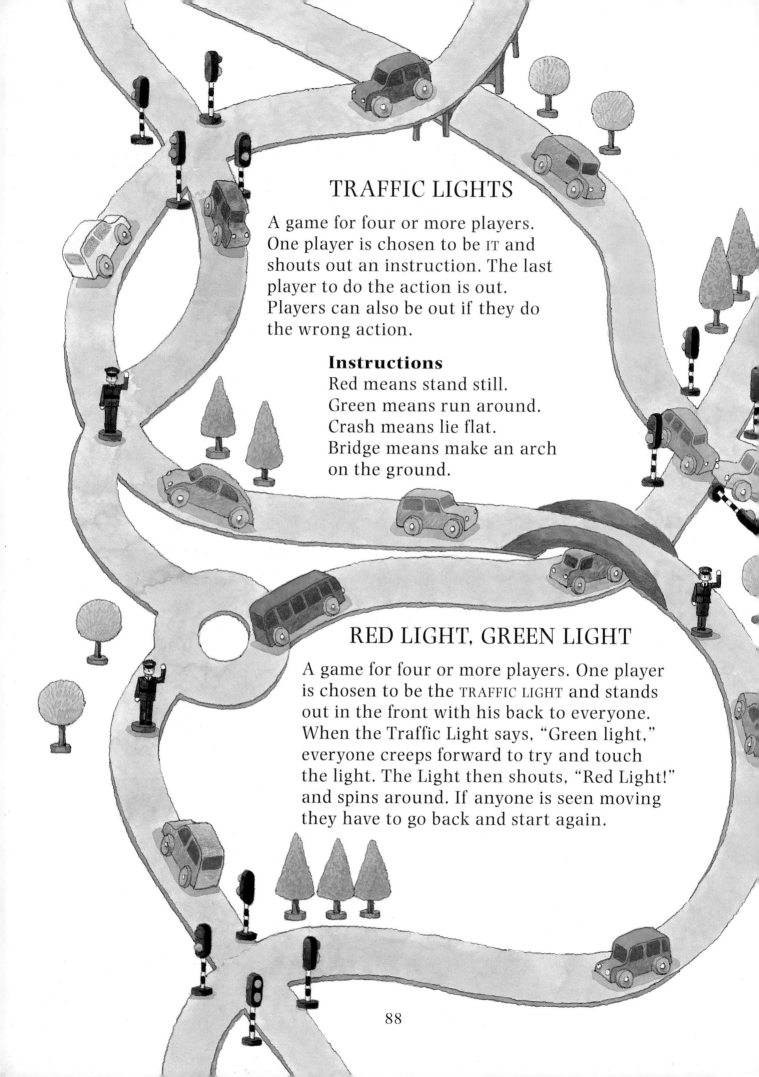

TRAFFIC LIGHTS

A game for four or more players. One player is chosen to be IT and shouts out an instruction. The last player to do the action is out. Players can also be out if they do the wrong action.

Instructions
Red means stand still.
Green means run around.
Crash means lie flat.
Bridge means make an arch on the ground.

RED LIGHT, GREEN LIGHT

A game for four or more players. One player is chosen to be the TRAFFIC LIGHT and stands out in the front with his back to everyone. When the Traffic Light says, "Green light," everyone creeps forward to try and touch the light. The Light then shouts, "Red Light!" and spins around. If anyone is seen moving they have to go back and start again.

INDEX OF RHYMES AND GAMES

T

U

W

Y

SUBJECT INDEX

GAMES FOR TEN PLAYERS AND MORE

GAMES FOR THE VERY YOUNG